JAMES DYER

TEACHING ARCHAEOLOGY IN SCHOOLS

SHIRE ARCHAEOLOGY

Cover illustration
A party of schoolchildren on a field visit to Hadrian's Wall.
(Photograph: James Dyer)

To N. B. L. for letting me teach it.

Published by
SHIRE PUBLICATIONS LTD
Cromwell House, Church Street, Princes Risborough,
Aylesbury, Bucks, HP17 9AJ, UK.

Series Editor: James Dyer

ISBN 0 85263 622 9

First published 1983

Set in 12 on 11 point Times roman
and printed in Great Britain by
C. I. Thomas & Sons (Haverfordwest) Ltd,
Press Buildings, Merlins Bridge, Haverfordwest.

Contents

Acknowledgements

Photographs are acknowledged as follows: Echo and Post Ltd, Hemel Hempstead, plate 3; Ole Malling, Historisk-Arkaeologisk Forsøgscenter, Lejre, Denmark, plates 14, 16-25, 27; Nordisk Pressefoto a/s, plate 15.

List of illustrations

1
Introduction

For a quarter of a century the writer has been teaching archaeology to children of all ages. During that time attitudes towards the subject have changed dramatically. More and more schools have found a place for it within the curriculum and the number of children studying for examinations has proliferated, as has the number of universities offering degrees in archaeology. In the early 1970s there were plenty of jobs to absorb the new interest, but at the time of writing the number of these has sadly declined.

Many friends have pressed me to write down my thoughts on the subject and this I have attempted to do in a few thousand words. This book is not a teaching manual. It is not intended to offer model lessons, but merely to act as a friendly guide to the pleasures and pitfalls of the subject, pointing out those ideas that I have found useful and offering warnings where the ground seems dangerous.

I have taken much care in choosing my illustrations and these are intended to supplement the text, each offering its own ideas for activities that can be followed by the enthusiastic teacher. Lack of space means that much has been left unsaid, and I shall be pleased to correspond with anyone who would like to develop a particular point.

During the preparation of this book I was lucky enough to spend some time with a group of children at the Lejre Archaeological Research Centre near Roskilde in Denmark. I am particularly indebted to the Centre's photographer, Ole Malling, for his hospitality and for providing me with pictures of the children at work there, and for giving me a number of ideas that I have used in my teaching. Most of the other photographs are my own and show former and present pupils getting involved in archaeology. I thank them all for their forbearance.

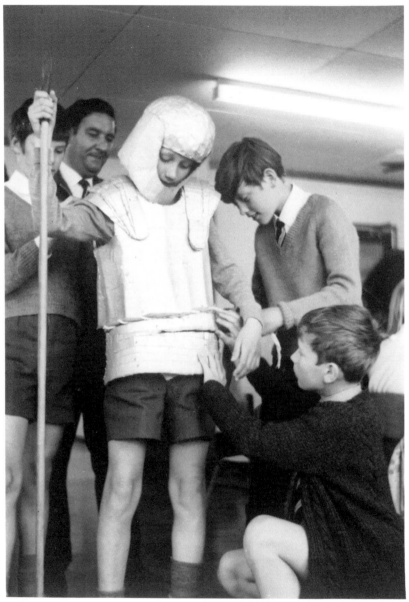

Plate 1. Eleven-year-old boys discover the intricacies of Roman armour by making a copy in cardboard.

2
The teacher

'Oh my friend, why do we waste our lives trying to teach?
Don't trouble to answer – I've already thought of several
answers!' *Gustav Holst.*

There is no reason why anyone with an interest in archaeology should
not attempt to teach it, provided that he has the ability to teach.
However, the more the teacher knows about the subject the more
successful he is likely to be. For the average teacher passing through a
Department of Education, scant attention is likely to have been paid
to the subject; consequently, in most cases, the teacher must turn
elsewhere for background knowledge. In the majority of cases this
must come from books and ultimately the school or local library,
where the collections may be somewhat sparse. The Council for
British Archaeology publishes a most useful booklist, and I have
given a brief selection of what I consider to be indispensable titles.

But what of the teacher for whom reading alone is not enough?
Here various evening or weekend courses should be considered. Local
reference libraries should have details of evening classes being held in
their district, some run by the local education authority, others by the
Workers' Educational Association or University Extension Courses.
There can be few areas where nothing is available. Local and national
museums also run courses of lectures and, if the teacher is convenient-
ly placed to reach London, then he should obtain the lists of lectures
held at the British Museum and similar institutions. Many teachers
will join the local archaeological society, and some may want to join
national societies that produce journals and winter lectures and study
tours. The Prehistoric Society, the Society for the Promotion of
Roman Studies and the Royal Archaeological Society all welcome
new members. A number of universities run weekend courses on
selected topics and details of these are usually available in the CBA
Calendar. The same publication contains information about excavations for the teacher who wishes to participate, although the local
museum or archaeological unit may be able to suggest one closer to
hand.

The best equipped teacher is probably one with a degree in
archaeology or an allied subject. Such people are rare in schools, and
may often have taken to teaching through frustration at trying to find
a full-time archaeological post. I would suggest that such teachers try

to work in a school with a sixth form where they may be permitted to teach the subject as part of a General Studies course, or even an examination subject. It is difficult to justify a place for archaeology on the timetable unless the teacher can promise the headmaster an examination result at the end of it; but most can be persuaded if they appreciate that they have a specialist on the staff who can offer something that the school next door does not do! The teacher, in justifying the subject, should also point out that an A/O or A level pass in archaeology is just as acceptable for university entrance as one in mathematics or domestic science. Parents will also be wary of the new subject at first, but once its value has been proved the defences will soon be down, and it becomes a source of family pride to say that 'Michael is doing archaeology at *his* school'. One will be asked what value it is to the child and again one will find it difficult to answer. One will offer platitudes about building for the future on a firm foundation of past knowledge. One will say that it is as useful as history or music, and one may be nearer the truth when one says that the child will develop a concern for his historical heritage and environment that should provide a lifelong interest.

Where a teacher is teaching at junior or middle school level a thorough knowledge of the subject is still necessary, though here reading is likely to be the teacher's main background support. If the archaeology is merely part of a series of history lessons then the amount of preparatory work may be minimal, but a term on prehistoric man will need more than a reading of Unstead! Detailed books on archaeology written specially for children may give the teacher sufficient guidance if they are up to date and accurate. Reference to the lists in the CBA *Archaeological Resources Handbook* will be helpful. Local archaeological society newsletters and journals will give up-to-date information on local excavations and discoveries, whilst it is well worth subscribing to *Current Archaeology* for details of national discoveries. I cannot stress too much that books are the essential tool for all archaeology teachers.

3
Beginnings

When should archaeology teaching begin? The answer must be: 'whenever the opportunity presents itself'. A simple question at an early age requires an honest answer, and every effort should be made to give it. By investing in a set of reputable encyclopaedias like the *Children's Britannica* the child who can read can be directed towards the correct answer: younger children can be read to.

In the infants' school archaeological questions may arise out of everyday occurrences like finding a piece of flint in the school garden, or seeing a skeleton in a museum or unearthed in a television programme. The astute teacher will draw on these experiences to talk in simple but intelligent terms about life in the past. Time, itself, will have little relevance to young children. They live from day to day, with birthdays and Christmas as the only reference points. Each teacher must know her own class and will judge the depth of teaching accordingly. Not only will periods of time run into each other, but different disciplines will overlap, especially palaeontology and anthropology. Even in the sixth form the boundaries of these subjects remain vague. It is no surprise for the archaeologist to be asked questions about fossils or aborigines. Certainly in the lower school we should not worry about these divisions.

Fossils are of enormous interest to young children. In most cases it is their first experience of something very old – 'thousands of years', though that still means very little. We can try to explain how fossils were formed and perhaps draw comparisons with casts of people from Pompeii in more recent times. Children will want to talk about dinosaurs and ice-age animals. There will be no differentiation in their minds in spite of a time gap of millions of years. Too many television films will have convinced them that men and dinosaurs were contemporaries, and perhaps it should be one of our major tasks in the earliest schools to disprove this hardy annual. Collecting fossils will appeal for a few days and a fossil table can be arranged with suitably labelled specimens on display. Young children love to get their tongues round such names as 'terebratula' or 'brachiopod', which they will remember and be able to spell long after they have forgotten 'February' or 'beautiful'.

But fossils are not archaeology. Scraps of pottery from a Romano-British farmstead may well turn up in the vicinity of the school, or a few medieval sherds from redevelopment in the town centre could find their way on to the display table. It is important that not only do the children handle this material but they also have an opportunity of seeing drawings of the type of vessel from which it came. Pictures of people in period costume will help to fit it into the appropriate background.

It may not be too early in the infant school to attempt models of caves built from piled-up stones or castles from cereal boxes as part of general interest lessons, but the more precise work will be reserved for the junior years when hands and intellects are better able to cope with craft work. Before leaving the infants, however, let us not belittle their enthusiasm. One school known to me encouraged its pupils to give talks about their hobbies in morning assembly. One seven-year-old produced twelve pages of notes, and drawings to pin on the wall, on the development of castles. Of course much of it had come from his encyclopaedia, but it was his enthusiasm that allowed him to hold his audience for fifteen minutes and answer their questions fluently.

Perhaps the best stimulant for infants is the teacher's own enthusiasm. If the teacher visits archaeological sites or takes part in digs then she will be able to enthuse about this and excite her class. Wall displays of her photographs, or a slide show, will convey something of what she has seen to the children, and they will eagerly question their parents or visit the library for more information.

Let me finish by referring to books for the very young. Some will be read to them, others they will read for themselves. Classes can always be stimulated by hearing a good story, whether it be fact or fiction, or a little of both. I have always found *Littlenose the Hunter* by John Grant a pleasing introduction to the world of stone age man. Children identify themselves with Littlenose and his attempts to make fire. Books for the children's own use are few. A search of my local library on one particular day found only two for the youngest children: *The First People* by T. A. Thompson (Blackwells, 1971), and *Forts and Castles* (Macdonald Starter, 1980). Ginn publish a useful series by the archaeologist Robin Place, called *First Interest Series – A Long Time Ago,* containing twelve books, with further titles on the way. One school librarian told me that she was constantly being asked for suitable books but had little to offer. Hardly anyone can write convincingly for children of five or six and, when they do, they are usually let down by their artists.

4
Juniors

Enthusiasm for learning develops to its fullest extent in the primary school. Up to the age of twelve or thirteen most children can be motivated to take an interest in almost anything and this is particularly true of archaeology. It is a subject that contains a strong element of discovery and mystery and this strengthens its appeal.

In the majority of junior schools archaeology will be introduced as an element in the history or local studies lesson. Most schools still tend to follow the nineteenth-century method of teaching history chronologically from the cave men in the first year to modern times in the final year. In this way the stuff of archaeology is taught to the youngest children, probably around eight years old, and does not get another airing in the junior school, so that at eleven when the child might enjoy being taught about prehistory, he is instead looking at the causes of the Second World War. Many teachers would feel that this is appropriate: the more complex study when the child is old enough to understand it. Yet prehistory can be complex too! The adequate and appropriate answer in primary schools seems to be the patch method of teaching, whereby the class studies different thematic topics every term or half-term, often jumping about chronologically from the Victorians to the Vikings. Criticism of this system is mainly based on the chronological confusion this may lead to in the child's mind, but there is little need to worry: few children develop a sense of time before the age of twelve, and they can all be helped to see things in order by the use of visual time lines in their exercise books or on the classroom walls.

There is a tendency to teach history in the primary school by means of stories, either of real characters, or by inventing people who represent what may have happened at a particular time. Since we do not know the name of the builder of Stonehenge we may invent a series of characters to suggest the use or construction of the henge monument. In teaching classical archaeology, either as part of a classics lesson or simply as tales of Greece and Rome, we have a wealth of myths and legends to draw upon. I still vividly remember forty years ago hearing how Hannibal crossed the Alps; and the work of Heinrich Schliemann in the discovery and excavation of Troy may well be an inspiration to some budding archaeologist of the future.

Plate 2. Caesar's invasion is brought to life in a pageant written and designed by eight-year-old children.

What is important for the teacher to realise is that he must know his source material thoroughly. If he is to bring a story alive, he must be able to draw on additional little details like the cauldron over the iron age fire to which daily additions were made for a perpetual stew, or the prevailing winds in the Bristol Channel that would make the sailing of rafts carrying Welsh stone for Stonehenge hazardous. Such details not only add to the authenticity of the story but aid the teacher when a difficult question is asked. Just as a teacher would hardly attempt to teach the use of log tables without some mathematical knowledge, so should he not attempt to teach early history without the necessary background knowledge. Where the teacher obtains that knowledge, I have already suggested.

The teacher who has sufficient confidence in his own knowledge may care to teach archaeology 'straight'. He will begin by talking about the subject: what it is and how it began. He will discuss how archaeologists obtain their information and the principles of stratigraphy and typology. There are no great secrets here to puzzle the intelligent youngster. A pile of books can represent soil layers or a collection of pens, from quill to ball point, can demonstrate typology.

The 'magic' of cropmarks on air photographs is clear to see and even proton magnetometers are not impossible to explain.

Teaching early history in depth will depend on the average ability of the class. Here one can get some surprises. I recall recently walking with trepidation into a group of late teenagers with leather jackets and motorcycles, who cheerfully recognised me and reminded me of a lesson on the Beaker Folk. They had been ten-year-olds in the lowest stream of a seven-stream school when I had taught them! Provided there is room on your timetable, then there is no reason why a chronological run-through of prehistory and classical archaeology should not be attempted, as long as you can convince your head teacher of its worth.

The pedants will tell us that teaching should not be all talk and chalk. There is much truth in this, but the teacher should also remember that there is little to beat a good story, well told, and those who are gifted with the ability to draw will find the blackboard indispensable for lightning sketches. Alternatively the picture may have been painstakingly drawn beforehand, copied from a book, traced from a slide or filmstrip, or published as a wallchart in one of the educational magazines. Whatever the source, the well informed

Plate 3. Experiments in building an iron age house end up like a scene from *Lord of the Flies,* but the children have learnt that such a house cannot be built in a few hours.

teacher will have checked the detail of the picture before using it. Stone age folk living in pit dwellings, or Stonehenge with an horizontal altar stone will not do. We must offer our children accuracy as far as possible.

There seems to be a certain futility in asking children to copy pictures, but there is no doubt that many enjoy this exercise, and it is a useful way of learning to draw. I have always preferred to persuade the children to try to see the subject from a different angle, or to combine a number of isolated elements – a quern, a group of pots, a loom – into a complete picture.

The greatest success can come from three-dimensional modelmaking and in the primary school this can develop to unlimited lengths. From modelling clay, cardboard and matchsticks and a host of other materials bronze age huts or iron age forts can be fashioned. Pieces of broken Marley tiles lend themselves to mosaic work and scraps of wool can be employed in weaving. Experimental archaeology like making flint tools or metal axes or firing pottery in kilns is all possible, but it needs very careful supervision. Flint is dangerously sharp and knapping requires safety goggles and leather gloves. Metal axes can be cast from molten solder, which presents a heat danger, also present with kilns. Only in exceptional circumstances is it possible for schools to build full-scale reproductions of prehistoric houses, though this can be done in a wooded rural environment. On such occasions children soon realise that houses cannot be built in an afternoon! A school with a high Victorian hall in Harpenden 'went Saxon' for a day. The hall became a Saxon hall with a central fireplace and benches around it. The children and staff made themselves Saxon-style clothes and ate a Saxon stew out of a large metal cauldron for lunch. They made drinking horns for milk, and after their meal listened to recorder-playing minstrels and storytellers. The floor of the hall was strewn with straw, and even a couple of dogs were invited to forage for scraps.

Visits to an archaeological site can be rewarding. It is important that the teacher should familiarise himself with it beforehand, so that he can offer an intelligible guided tour of the monument, unless an official guide is to be employed. In the latter case it is to be hoped that the person can direct the information to a level which the children can follow readily, yet not feel that they are being talked down to. The comment that 'she talked to us like real people' is a sure sign that the children appreciated what they heard. The best kind of sites to visit are upstanding monuments like hillforts or castles, where the children need only a little imagination to bring them to life. Travelling twenty miles to see a round barrow is not very inspiring (unless you can get

Plate 4. Storming a hillfort, an exercise that sorts out the men from the boys.

inside it), but even there the careful interpretation of the excavation report may make even a grassy mound into an object of fascination. With hillforts and castles the children can become involved in the function of the site. Try storming them, by climbing up the steepest approach. Work out how the entrance could be defended. Seek out the nearest water supply. All this persuades the child to see himself in the role of the original inhabitant.

Children love to be taken to see excavations, but they rapidly become bored. There is nothing more baffling than to stare into a muddy trench for the first time and be told that you are looking at a third-century occupation layer. The most patient site director has difficulty in explaining his findings to experts, and to expect ten-year-olds to understand what they are seeing is asking a lot. Burial mounds and cemeteries are perhaps the easiest kinds of site to follow, but the strata of a medieval town site take more effort than the average schoolchild can muster. It has become the practice on some sites to appoint a full-time officer with responsibility for talking to parties of visitors. Such people have to be able to switch from eight-year-olds to senior citizens a dozen times a day. At one famous site the lady appointed to talk to school parties failed miserably: she did not like children and had no rapport with them. 'Don't touch that' was her most frequent remark, and yet touching was essential to get the feel of the site.

Physical contact with ancient objects is one of the most important aspects of archaeology teaching. Bridging the gap of two thousand years between the present day and the Roman who first handled a coin or made a pot can be a thrilling experience for the imaginative child, although there will always be those for whom the experience does nothing. Many museums provide objects which children can handle, and enquiry at your local museum should soon tell you if they are willing to co-operate by loaning objects or arranging handling sessions. Some teachers have their own collections of objects which they have bought from dealers or have been given from unknown sites. It is possible to obtain pieces of Romano-British pottery from a museum or excavation once it has been documented, since it is found in such large quantities that it is seldom all kept. Never, however, should the teacher try digging into sites in an effort to obtain material of his own, since, together with the use of metal detectors, it is tantamount to looting, is invariably against the law and demonstrates a total lack of understanding of the basic principles of the science of archaeology. A number of museums produce facsimiles of their objects, and a collection of these can prove invaluable in the classroom.

The nearest that many children will get to excavation and handling objects is in the sport of field walking. Here, with the landowner's permission, lines of children will progress across a freshly ploughed field, eyes glued to the ground, looking for signs of ancient activity: a piece of pottery or tile, a scrap of metal, an area of burning. Such activity is marked with a stick and the exact position of each object recorded on a plan of the field and placed in a labelled bag. Such walking across a series of fields can build up a picture of areas of ancient activity and will often correlate with information from aerial photographs or medieval parish surveys. The results should be passed on to the local museum or archaeological unit. The chief disadvantage of field walking is that it can seldom be attempted by whole classes of children: farmers flinch at the sight of an army of youngsters, marching across their freshly ploughed fields. It is best reserved for small 'out of school' groups like archaeology clubs and societies. Abusing the system with a group of unruly children often prevents legitimate workers from visiting the fields.

5
Secondary

All the primary school activities can be continued in greater depth into the secondary school. In many cases the historical cycle, prehistoric to modern times, begins all over again, with emphasis on post-1485 for examination purposes. Ancient times are often chosen for topic work and individual projects can result. Again archaeology is frequently the handmaid of history, although greater emphasis may be placed on local studies or environmental studies. The archaeology of the local area may be examined in considerable detail. A lot will depend on what published material is available, whether there is a local museum with information, or a local archaeologist who is ready to give his time and knowledge to the teacher and possibly the children too. The amount of available information varies enormously. If you teach in an historic city or a chalk downland parish you are likely to have plenty of archaeological material fairly close at hand, but a rural school in a clay vale or a new town on the salt flats may have little of traditional archaeological interest to offer, although there may be possibilities in the field of so-called 'industrial archaeology', which is really the province of the economic historian.

Secondary age children are better able to appreciate visiting field monuments and seeing them both as historical features and as tangible objects which can be surveyed mathematically, described in poetry, drama and prose, drawn and modelled. An in-depth survey of a local earthwork or ruin can make a stimulating theme for a local history display, providing that such a site is within easy reach. If not, it may have to be described by proxy: books, charts, slides, films and filmstrips can all be used to study a monument such as Stonehenge, perhaps culminating in a long coach trip to complete the study, and the work can be finally presented as a wall display, class book or visual and dramatic presentation. Where mathematics has been used to make accurate measured surveys of the site, copies should be deposited in the local museum, record office or archaeological sites and monuments record.

The archaeology teacher in the secondary school is either going to teach the subject as part of another discipline or, if he is lucky enough to have archaeology on the timetable, it will almost certainly be aimed

Plate 5. An experiment with stratification. The layers of soil show clearly in a glass bowl.
Plate 6. The effect of disturbance on stratification.

towards an examination. Teaching towards exams is discussed in the next chapter. Here let us consider teaching archaeology as a general study, to widen the child's horizon. Where do we start? In no subject are we better qualified to take Alice's advice and 'begin at the beginning'. But where is that? Do we start with the first toolmakers in Africa? Do we start with the origins of agriculture in the Near East? Do we begin with the first human remains in Britain, or our own locality? Or do we consider the methods and techniques of archaeologists? All are possible, but the teacher will have his own ideas, and these will depend on his own interests and strengths.

I can perhaps do best by describing a few of the methods known to me:

Human origins

Here the teacher begins by describing theories for the origin of the earth and man. In a multiracial class these may come from the children, but such beliefs as those of the Eskimos, the Egyptians or the Vikings might be discussed, to be followed by the biblical account in Genesis. Each is analysed in detail and similarities are sought. The current scientific explanations are given and Darwin's theory of evolution introduced. From this, anthropological accounts of the development of man are examined and the emergence of *Homo habilis, erectus,* Neanderthal and *sapiens.* The physical appearance and material equipment of each group is examined, and famous discoveries by anthropologists and archaeologists are studied in detail.

The agricultural revolution

The teacher observes that one place where early cereals, sheep and cattle all occur in their wild state together is the mountainous region of modern Turkey. The move from nomadic hunting and gathering to collecting wild grasses and keeping animals is described, and various ideas are discussed to explain the domestication process. With the control of pests and animals man could lead a settled existence and so permanent settlements developed, leading to the first villages and towns of the Fertile Crescent. The diffusionists would see the spread of farming from Anatolia south-eastwards into Mesopotamia and Egypt, and westwards through the Mediterranean islands or up the Danube into Europe and eventually Britain. Others seek independent development from a number of centres.

Prehistoric Britain

This is so vast a subject that it can be presented in various ways. Either it can involve a direct chronological account of early man in

Plate 7. A well thought-out worksheet calls for concentration in Chesters Museum, Northumberland.

Britain as a whole, or in the school's locality, or particular topics can be examined, such as homes, agriculture, warfare or religion. This will depend on the teacher's own interest and knowledge. A number of recent textbooks adopt the chronological approach and are readily available to teachers. The thematic treatment was best demonstrated by Grahame Clark in his book *Prehistoric England,* first published in 1940, but available in more recent paperback editions (Batsford).

Roman Britain and the Dark Ages

Much of what I have said in the previous paragraph applies here. Roman Britain is exceptionally well catered for in a wealth of books at all levels, some of which are listed in the bibliography. The Dark Ages are less well covered and are probably best left to the teacher with a specialist interest.

Archaeological methods

An explanation of what archaeology is about is followed by a brief historical introduction outlining the main developments in the history of archaeology. This leads on to such topics as how archaeologists obtain their information, how they know where to dig, and how old sites and objects are, including scientific methods of dating. Consideration is given to preservation and how objects and sites can be conserved, followed by how such material is presented to both specialists and the public. The work of such bodies as the Department of the Environment, the Royal Commission on Historical Monuments, the Council for British Archaeology, and national and local museums can all be looked at and appropriate visits made.

Foreign archaeology

The archaeology of France and western Europe offers much that is attractive but tends to be neglected, except for cave art. Special lessons in connection with foreign visits might be considered. The most obvious areas for study here are the civilisations of Greece and Rome, both of which are dealt with at length by schools studying classics. Egypt is always popular and is well documented and displayed at the British Museum. Central America has its adherents and in recent years topics such as China have occasionally found their way into schools, inspired no doubt by the discovery of the pottery army of Emperor Shi-Huang-Di.

Industrial archaeology

Better described as historical archaeology, this subject looks at the material remains of the historical past. It has a tendency to concentrate on industrial and transport history, but any aspect of the past that can be illuminated by the archaeological approach is a worthy topic. It is particularly useful for urban schools, where documentary evidence can be used to supplement our knowledge of derelict factories, railways, canals and a host of other structures.

Plate 8. Field walking reveals a thick scatter of stones and bricks and the site of a well belonging to an Elizabethan house.

Plate 9. Not only sight, but touch is also important in appreciating archaeological material such as a mosaic pavement.

6
Examinations

Archaeology is not an essential subject like English or mathematics. It would not matter if it was never mentioned in schools; a national strike of archaeologists would not bring the country to its knees. It is taught in a few schools because groups of enlightened teachers feel that it helps to extend the quality of life in the same way that history or art will do. However, if it is taught in its own right, then it has to justify its existence. It has to be examined. Mathematicians have to be able to measure its success in terms of statistics. It has to hold its own with geography and classics, and prove that it can be used as a qualifying exam for those seeking university entrance. If a headmaster can offer it at 'A' level in his sixth form, or even at CSE or A/O level, then he is likely to support its teaching. If he does not see it as a prestige examination subject, then it is likely to get pushed into a General Studies course, and little money will be spent on library books essential to the subject.

Certificate of Secondary Education
   Archaeology can be a happy choice of subject for CSE. Sometimes it is called local archaeology, archaeological studies or industrial archaeology, depending on the whim and ability of its teacher. There is no CSE Mode 1 and so all archaeological exams are Mode 3. The standards of these examinations vary enormously throughout Britain. Some examiners require single-word answers to long strings of questions: 'What is the archaeological name for the new stone age?'; 'Name a hillfort in our area.' Others require essay-type answers comparable to those set for the A/O level. Unfortunately the Mode 3 exams have local moderators and there is no national standard as there is in the A/O level exam. For the examination to have real value this problem urgently needs solving. The East Anglian Board seems to have been the only one to propose a Mode 1 examination, but so few schools showed an interest in it that the idea was dropped.
   As I have said above, the choice of name and syllabus content for the CSE will depend on the individual teacher, who will plan it according to his own strengths. When he leaves the school, a new teacher may inherit something he cannot continue or has to alter drastically. Since the teacher also plans his own examination paper, it is inevitable that his teaching will be biased to those sections of the

syllabus that he knows will be examined; so again this tends to degrade the value that can be placed on the final result.

From these comments it may be felt that I do not like the CSE examinations. To some extent this is true, for often they tend to prostitute the value of our subject. However, a syllabus that is carefully planned can be just as rewarding for the pupils as an A/O level for the more able. Moreover, the CSE is intended for those less able to cope with more academic work. But archaeology *is* a very academic subject. Its terminology and its concepts are highly technical, but I have always found that carefully taught and given sufficient time the subject can be mastered by those who are often considered incapable of examination success. We have one strong point in our favour: our subject has an air of mystery and excitement about it which appeals to less able children, and if we teach it well we can hold their attention indefinitely, especially if we can introduce a practical element into our lessons. As I have already said, each syllabus varies according to the teacher, but a model Mode 1 syllabus has been prepared by the CBA Schools Committee and is obtainable on request. This can be used as the basis for any Mode 3 and is already in use in a number of schools.

The Alternative Ordinary Level

There are two A/O level examinations available, one from London University and the other from the Joint Matriculation Board (addresses in chapter 12). Whilst both cover the methods and principles of archaeology in Paper 1, the London Board then offers in Paper 2 a wide range of questions on British archaeology from the palaeolithic to the post-medieval period, with a choice of special topics in a third paper ranging over twelve optional aspects of world archaeology. As an alternative to Paper 2 the London Board will accept an individual study based on local fieldwork. The second part of the Joint Matriculation Board examination is concerned with the archaeology of Roman Britain, though material used in Paper 1 may be drawn from the neolithic to post-Roman period. Both Boards offer lists of suggested books which are helpful when planning the course, though it is unlikely that any school library could stock more than a handful of them. Few suitable textbooks exist and most schools have very little money to purchase any. As a result the teacher is called upon to prepare and duplicate his own information sheets or to photocopy (illegally) from existing books.

Since the examination is at A/O level it is clear that the examiners have in mind candidates in the sixth form and colleges of higher education, studying beyond O level, as well as adults who may be following an evening course and would like some kind of qualification. However, I have found the London examination quite suitable for good fourteen to sixteen year-olds working for O levels. There may even be some competition with students wanting to take history *or* archaeology, and occasionally the two syllabuses can duplicate material (e.g. origins of farming), which makes it a little tedious for a student following both subjects.

The Cambridge Advanced Level
This is the ultimate examination before beginning a university course. Indeed the standard is set by direct comparison with the former first-year tripos course at Cambridge. It began as long ago as 1947 when Miles Burkitt, Glyn Daniel and F. W. Kuhlicke prepared the first mock paper. It is now the best established examination and has followed a more or less predictable pattern from the beginning. Its link to the university course makes it a difficult paper to teach, since the tutor has to be in touch with the latest university thinking. What is more, it has to be the Cambridge school of thought! This raises once again the problem of the teacher keeping up to date. Ideas in archaeology change so rapidly that no sooner is a new book published than it is out of date. Libraries are finding it more and more difficult to buy the latest books, and teachers' salaries are unlikely to

Plate 10. Students on a field excursion consider the function of a hypocaust.

stretch in that direction, when, for example, the standard work on the lower and middle palaeolithic was priced in 1981 at £35.00. The Schools Committee of the CBA can go a little way to helping keep teachers up to date, but it cannot provide summaries of the latest books and thinking (except in the briefest outline in *Archaeological Abstracts)*. This can only come from the teacher, who must display dedication and willingness to consult archaeological libraries at the universities or Society of Antiquaries. The latter library can be consulted by non-Fellows, provided they belong to the Royal Archaeological Institute, though they may not borrow books (membership through the Assistant Secretary, Royal Archaeological Institute, 304 Addison House, Grove End Road, London NW8 9EL).

Most examination papers are planned two years ahead, and the assiduous archaeology teacher will keep a note of current trends to try to predict the sort of questions likely to be set. The A level syllabus is only a rough guide, particularly to Section A, and fringe subjects have a habit of appearing that are only broadly within its scope. Rescue units and Marxism have both been mentioned in recent papers. Even so there is plenty of scope for the well informed student provided he is willing to work. Perhaps the most difficult aspect of the

Plate 11. Even in pouring rain old legends must be checked: counting the Rollright stones.

A level is the project. This is chosen, preferably with a local connection, and describes museum objects or local sites in some detail. In some cases a great deal of effort goes into making accurate drawings of objects or surveys of sites, often completely original work, and one wonders if the examiners take this into account, when compared with the work of students who have regurgitated published accounts for the umpteenth time. In schools where a number of candidates are entered each year, it is inevitable that the range of subjects runs out and has to be repeated, which must be tedious for both the examiners and the teachers.

Topics for A level projects tend to fall into two groups, narrative and analytical. The first gives a straightforward account of a site or subject which may be good in its way, but tends to rely on published sources and offers little that is new or the pupil's own work. The analytical approach is much more suitable for A level work and allows the writer greater freedom of expression and almost forces him to examine material and formulate an opinion of his own. Descriptions of sites are always popular with the less able, especially if the student has easy access to one, and plenty of information. Some, like Stonehenge and Avebury, have become hackneyed, and 'Earthworks of the Ridgeway' or 'Hillforts of the Peak District' are much more acceptable. The best topics involve original research either using museum objects, field walking and surveying, or recording buildings or tombstones. This gives the student the best opportunity to show that he is familiar with the subject matter. 'Saxon brooches of the Norwich area', 'Celtic coins of the Catuvellauni' or the 'Moated sites of south Buckinghamshire' are all acceptable. The examiners are likely to be less happy about topics where the student has limited access to the source material, like the 'Temples of Malta' or even 'Scottish brochs' (when he lives in the south of England). Town studies can be valuable, but the teacher should be wary of the fine lines to be drawn between archaeology, history and historical geography.

Books, maps and aerial photographs are even more essential tools for A level work. Not only does the candidate need access to the basic texts, including national and local archaeological periodicals, but for the projects he will need a detailed local collection as well. Museums and libraries may be able to help, and school libraries might build up a collection of photocopies and newspaper cuttings. At the time of writing A level students need basic textbooks valued at about £15 per head, plus at least a further £20 per head on library books.

No university cites A level archaeology as an entry qualification for those contemplating a university course in archaeology or anthropology, but students who have taken the A level at school have invariably reported that it provided an excellent foundation for their university studies, and that they found themselves in a strongly advantageous position over their companions.

If children study archaeology at school a few will want to consider it as a career. Teachers will be asked for advice, and the kindest is probably to say 'don't'. Job opportunities are so few that hundreds of students find themselves without satisfactory employment. However, the persistent student will not be put off, nor should be. What he will want to know is what A level subjects to take for a career in archaeology. This is difficult to answer. It depends on the ability of the child and in what branch of archaeology the student is going to specialise. Geography can be most useful, particularly if the course is fairly traditional with plenty of physical background, although modern geographical thinking, involving central place theories and the like, is crucial to the new archaeology as well. Many youngsters will consider history, but not if the course concentrates on modern political history: social history has more to offer. Art can be invaluable to the archaeologist, and so can technical drawing. All the sciences have something to offer, particularly if the student is interested in environmental archaeology. For choice I would single out biology first, followed by physics. Computer studies are playing a larger and larger role in archaeological research and a knowledge of the basic principles of computer planning might save the student a lot of time during his university career. Latin and Greek are necessary for anyone contemplating classical archaeology, and modern languages make it possible to read some of the vast amount of foreign literature available: French and German are equally useful. Some universities require a modern language.

Without a good degree in archaeology there is little prospect of employment. Youngsters who have a CSE Grade 1 pass in the subject and nothing more, except a burning enthusiasm, are likely to be disappointed. Their activity is likely to be confined to the local archaeological society. As a hopeful tailpiece I mention one old student of mine whose determination got him the career he wanted through the side door. On leaving school with a CSE Grade 1 he took a higher education course in photography and specialised in archaeology: now he is a very successful site photographer.

7
Visual aids

In archaeology the visual element is most important and teachers will need to build up collections of slides and pictures. Many commercial sets of slides are available and can be bought from the Department of the Environment and most museums. A number of filmstrips made by Visual Publications, Longmans and similar firms can be cut up and made into slides, and the teacher should always look out for advertisements in educational publications that may mention appropriate material. It is quite likely that the slides the teacher really requires are not available. This need not stop the enterprising teacher who is prepared to make his own slides, either by going out into the countryside and taking the necessary pictures, or by copying them from a book, magazine or postcard. Manufacturing one's own slides is very simple provided one has the basic equipment. This may require an expensive outlay at first, but it is well worth it in the long run. It consists of a single-lens reflex camera with interchangeable lenses and a set of extension tubes. These latter allow the photographer to get extremely close to the picture being copied, filling the screen with a postage stamp for example. Whilst a copying easel is useful, it is not absolutely essential. The picture to be copied is best placed in strong daylight and can be copied in colour on any reversal film or in black-and-white on Agfa Dia-Direct film. The Dia-Direct film is particularly suitable for black-and-white diagrams. Pictures in books are protected by copyright, but provided they are not used outside the classroom little harm is done, and most archaeologists assume that their drawings will be made into slides for teaching purposes. Intricate drawings in coloured chalk on a clean blackboard can be recorded on colour slide film and projected whenever the teacher needs to repeat them. Such slides have a luminous quality which is very pleasing.

The teacher who photographs using colour print films will find the results less useful, since the small size of the prints makes them less easy for a class to view as a whole. Similarly, buying picture postcards of a site is useful for showing to small groups or for copying on to slide film when you get home, but they are too small for most practical purposes. However, postcards and prints should not be scorned: carefully filed in a shoebox, they can be used for reference by students researching a particular topic, like mosaics or Greek vases.

Plate 12. Field sketching at the Nympsfield long barrow.

Large coloured pictures from educational magazines and colour supplements may be suitable for wall display, but if the picture is an imaginative reconstruction it should be checked for accuracy. I would encourage teachers to build up a reference collection of such pictures, so that displays can be mounted, even at short notice.

Aerial photographs will be an essential item in the archaeology classroom. Slide sets produced by Aerofilms or Archaeological Advisers will be useful for class viewing, but individual photographs of famous or local sites will also be needed for familiarisation. In the A/O level examination children are required to answer questions about an aerial photograph. I would suggest that the school buys some good quality photographs from the Cambridge University Collection, Aerofilms, the Ashmolean Museum or one of the other commercial organisations. Alternatively a book such as D. N. Riley's *Aerial Archaeology in Britain* (Shire Archaeology) contains many useful pictures at a reasonable price.

Ordnance Survey maps are an indispensable tool of our trade, and the A/O level examination includes a map extract. Whilst sets of two or three specimen areas will be necessary, especially for use in mock examinations, it may also be possible to come to an arrangement with your geography department to share sets of maps of archaeologically rich areas. Teachers will also be interested in the larger scale Ordnance Survey plans of earthworks in their neighbourhood, and some of these should be available to students, especially if they are doing local project work. The Ordnance Survey period maps of *Roman Britain, Dark Age Britain* and *Southern Britain in the Iron Age* will also be necessary items in the archaeology department, preferably linen-mounted on rollers for ease of use. Library copies will also be valuable.

It is possible to hire a small but useful group of archaeological films. The *Archaeological Resources Handbook* lists these and gives details of companies supplying them. The films are also being supplemented by video-cassette material. Perhaps the great advantage of using film is that children can study situations that are not usually available to them, like excavation. Barry Cunliffe's work at Danebury is described in *Digging up Man,* and the story of an excavation in West Yorkshire is well told and illustrated in *Dalton Parlours.* Reconstructing the prehistoric past is particularly difficult, but it is sensibly done in *Cave Dwellers of the Stone Age,* now more than twenty years old. Dating techniques are clearly explained in *Archaeological Dating: Retracing Time,* an American film. All these films are suitable for secondary age groups. Most schools now own video-recorders and, in spite of the doubtful legality of the matter, will probably record suitable television series for classroom use. Programmes like the excellent *Making of Mankind* will be obvious choices here. The cassette tape recorder will also be used for recording sound radio programmes like *Origins* when the material is appropriate. These make excellent discussion topics and can usefully be stored and played when the teacher is absent through illness.

Replicas of archaeological objects are obtainable from a number of museums and occasionally from small short-lived companies. Since it is difficult, and indeed seldom desirable, to obtain originals, the replicas are the next best thing, and some of them like the Bush

Plate 13. Students discussing the blocked entrance at Belas Knap.

Barrow dagger from Devizes Museum are very realistic indeed. Enterprising teachers may attempt to make their own replicas, borrowing spare objects from museums, and either using plaster of Paris or the more versatile fibre glass and other plastics available in school workshops today. Handling good replicas helps the pupils to become familiar with the main types of objects met in archaeological contexts, and with sufficient examples from different museums exercises in typology can be tried out. They are also useful in learning to draw the shapes of typical specimens. Pottery is particularly difficult to draw, but reproducing the shape of pots is very important in archaeology. I found good drawings and photographs of typical beakers and collared urns and persuaded my local village potter to make me replicas. Some of these are whole pots, made at slightly under actual size, and some have been cut into two halves. The children can lay the halves on a sheet of paper and draw round them to get very accurate shapes. The half pots are also useful when trying to explain the archaeological method of drawing pottery. The replica pots are hard baked and could not be mistaken for the original material.

Plate 14. Replicas of iron age costumes and pottery loaned to schools by a Danish archaeological centre, before children make a field visit.

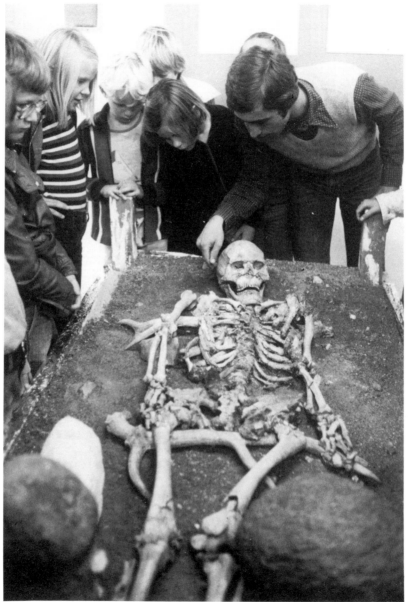

Plate 15. The fascination of a skeleton. The remains of a mesolithic huntsman can be brought to 'life' again with the aid of a sympathetic teacher.

8
Field visits

Field visits are amongst the most popular and rewarding archaeological activities and should be encouraged wherever possible. They may range from a half-day excursion to the nearest barrow group to a week in some distant part of Britain or abroad.

Within ten minutes drive from my school is a small promontory fort which is ideal when discussing methods of defence and potential function of the site. Unfortunately we cannot dash to it whenever we feel inclined, as the County Education Office has to be informed of all visits fourteen days ahead for insurance purposes. However, with this proviso in mind, and always depending on transport being available, an afternoon spent on the windy hilltop helps the children appreciate the stamina and determination of the fort builders and their would-be attackers.

Of all visits to archaeological sites in Britain, the one favoured by most schools will be the Avebury and Stonehenge trip. Schools from all over the Midlands and the south of England plan this as a one-day visit, whilst others from further afield stay at the Salisbury Youth Hostel. On my own excursions we commence at Avebury, with a guided tour of the stone circle and museum. The bank of the earthwork makes a fine grandstand and a good place to eat sandwiches. If you have plenty of time it is worth including the climb up to Windmill Hill. Next we progress down the Kennet Avenue and make our way to the lay-by on the A4 east of Silbury Hill. Allowing an hour we take the signposted walk to the West Kennett long barrow and view Silbury Hill from a distance. Having turned our coach round at Beckhampton we drive east along the A4 for four miles until we approach Fyfield. Before entering the village we turn right (south) to Lockeridge, where on the southern edge of the village, at the Dene, is one of the best sources of sarsen stone still lying in its natural position. The road proceeds south-west crossing Wansdyke, with clear views of Knap Hill causewayed camp on the left and Adam's Grave long barrow on the right. At Alton Barnes we turn right (west) for Devizes, passing the site of All Cannings Cross. Devizes Museum is essential for all archaeologists, and at least an hour can be profitably spent there, before proceeding south again to Stonehenge. If time allows it is worth following the A360 as far as the Winter-bourne Stoke roundabout, to view the extensive barrow group beside the road. The tour can then return to the A344 and Stonehenge itself.

Stonehenge is one of the big disappointments of archaeology for children. They grow up with the notion that it is an enormous group of stones dominating Salisbury Plain, only to find a tiny group of grey blocks huddled some distance away behind a rope, where it is difficult to see all the architectural refinements that they should have heard about. It is a good idea to have binoculars available for detailed study. If time allows it is worth getting away from the crowds to visit the Normanton barrow group, a mile to the south, or Woodhenge and Durrington Walls three miles north-east. Old Sarum and Salisbury Museum are no great distance away, but all this is too much for one day and is better spread over a weekend.

If possible, five school days or a week are to be preferred. I like to introduce archaeology to my A/O level children with five days in the Cotswolds (including travelling). I do this at the beginning of their course, when they have almost no background knowledge, but I find it invaluable later when I want them to visualise a particular type of site. I begin (for convenience) with a visit to the Rollright Stones, which I use as an example of the mixture of fact and fantasy that surrounds many ancient sites. I use the Painswick Beacon to introduce hillforts and to show how sites have suffered in the past from industrial activity. This is a good site to try 'storming' — a race up the ramparts will subdue a boisterous group for half an hour! On Selsley Common, south of Stroud, we examine a damaged long barrow, with obvious robbers' pit, but no sign of a burial chamber. This makes a useful introduction to the Cotswold barrows, because we then move on three miles south-west to the Nympsfield long barrow, recently restored, but lacking a roof, so that its cruciform plan can be clearly seen. A mile further south is Hetty Pegler's Tump, a barrow complete with roof and locked modern door. A key can be obtained from further down the road, and a torch is absolutely essential. Uleybury hillfort, close by, can be completely walked around and offers spectacular views, as well as impressing with the great strength of its site.

Another Cotswold day is devoted to Belas Knap, Cleeve Cloud hillfort, Leckhampton hillfort and Crickley Hill fort. Chedworth villa and Cirencester museum, amphitheatre and city walls also make a worthwhile day.

An alternative field week can be spent in Cumbria and Northumbria. Youth hostels, out of season, offer excellent accommodation at very reasonable prices. I spend two days studying Hadrian's Wall, and two days looking at prehistoric sites. The whole tour is carefully introduced beforehand: I have learnt from long experience that it is no fun trying to point out the layout of a Roman

Plate 16. To understand the past we must experience it for ourselves. Children experiment with a horse-drawn plough.

Plate 17. Using a replica of a prehistoric ard. How many horsepower is represented by a group of enthusiastic children?

fort in the pouring rain or driving snow! My excursion is planned to build up to a climax, and I commence by noticing how the Wall has been destroyed, and we observe the reuse of stone at Lanercost Priory. We then inspect Banks Turret (T 52A) and the view to the south. At Appletree (595656) it is possible to see the line of the turf wall. Birdoswald fort is scarcely worth a view, but the section of Wall immediately east as far as Milecastle 49 should be visited, if only for its inscriptions (identified by metal tags low down in the wall) and the high view of Willowford bridge crossing. Moving on to Gilsland school, we then walk along a good section of Wall to Willowford bridge, and back to the Poltross Burn milecastle (MC 48). East of Greenhead is the new Roman Army Museum, which is worth a visit before facing the dramatic Walltown Crags, one of the finest surviving stretches of the whole Wall. Vindolanda, with its excavated village street, its reconstructed section of Hadrian's Wall and Interval Tower, its fort, its excellent museum, its Roman milestone and its commercialism, is worth at least two hours.

To get the feel of the Wall the walk from Steel Rigg to Housesteads is essential, especially on a clear, crisp morning. Although it is the wildest part of the Wall it is also the most used, and you are seldom alone, even on the coldest New Year's Day. It is worth drawing the attention of the children to the erosion that is taking place, due to

Plate 18. Experimental digging using antler and stone picks.

Plate 19. Cutting corn by hand using a metal sickle.

over visiting, and they might consider how best to combat it. Housesteads fort and museum, Carrawbrough with its Mithras temple and Chesters fort and museum can all be fitted into this day.

One of my Cumbrian days is devoted to prehistory and starts with the stone circle of Long Meg and Her Daughters and the ruins of the Little Meg cairn with its decorated stones. South of Penrith are the two henge monuments of King Arthur's Round Table and Mayburgh. A journey beside Ullswater for light relief and a climb to Aira Force lead eventually to the most attractive of all lakeland sites, the Castlerigg stone circle. Returning through Carlisle a stop at the museum is very worthwhile. A further day is spent in Northumbria, visiting hillforts and smaller sites. A good exercise in map reading begins with a search for the Goatstones stone circle, a little four poster (NY 828747). We then make for Rothbury Forest calling at Lordenshaws hillfort, noticing the two nearby stones bearing rock carvings (NU 055993); further along the same minor road is Tossonburgh fort (NU 023005) and Harehaugh (NT 970998), with a small enclosure clearly visible beyond the road to the south-east, and splendid meanders of the river Coquet to the north. Alnham Castle hillfort is also worth a visit (NT 980109).

Visiting archaeological sites abroad is much more demanding. I have tried three areas with varying success, Brittany and the Dordogne area of France, and Denmark. Without a doubt Denmark is the ideal country for the archaeological student. Its larger museums have labels in English as well as Danish, and excellent English guidebooks are available at a number of sites. A typical day would be to visit Roskilde on Zealand with its Viking Ship Museum, where the boats recovered from the Roskilde fjord are being restored in front of the public gaze, and where there is detailed information in English on the Vikings and their boats. The cathedral is worth a visit, before travelling 8 kilometres (5 miles) south-west to Øm, where there is a great barrow with room for twenty people in its stone burial chamber (torches essential). 5 kilometres (3 miles) further west is the Historical Archaeological Research Centre at Lejre, open daily from May to September, with its reconstructed iron age village, and experiments in agriculture, weaving, smelting, pottery making and so on. Classes of Danish children are taught at the Centre, either residentially for a week or for a whole-day or three-hour visit. English parties can sometimes be fitted in, but there is much local demand. The Butser Ancient Farm Project in Hampshire is the nearest thing to Lejre in England.

Wherever visits are made, meticulous planning is essential. It is not enough to look up sites on a map and in a guidebook. The teacher should visit them beforehand and look for the snags: the bull in the field at Lordenshaws, the museum closed for alterations. Problems like this can be overcome with preparation. The teacher must also know the archaeological history and features of the site, unless a local guide is being employed, and he should work out beforehand where the best viewpoints are situated and how best to make a point clearly, relishing any little titbit of information that will bring some aspect of the site alive. For the most successful visits, the teacher has to work hard, doing most of the preparation himself. Do not leave jobs to others. If you want to make sure the coach is booked, book it yourself. If you are wondering where you can park the coach, telephone the local police and ask them. Only in this way can you hope to experience peace of mind and a contented group of children.

9
Museum experience

Archaeologists live in a very specialised world, and sometimes it is hard for them to present their ideas to the public. This is made easier if the public can be introduced to those ideas when they are young, either in the classroom or through museums. Although many museums are preoccupied with caring for their collections there are fortunately many in Britain that will cater for young people and prepare special displays for them, or will enable children to handle material, or offer a talk about objects in the collection. A number of books have been written on using museums and I will not duplicate much of what they say here, but it is essential for archaeology teachers to know their local museum and its collections thoroughly, including material not on public display, as well as the visible contents of national museums.

Visits to museums should be a regular part of the archaeology lesson. If the teacher has any say in planning his timetable he might ask for a halfday block of time each week, which can be used for visits and will not cut across other teachers' lessons. Children should learn to discriminate between good and bad museum displays and should try to decide why their local museum is, or is not, in the *Good Museums Guide* (Papermac). They can begin by asking themselves how well the museum caters for them. Are the cases attractively laid out with clear labels that they can understand, placed at a suitable height for them to read? Does the label suggest where more advanced pupils can find further information? Does the arrangement of the exhibits make them want to linger and learn more? Is there a workroom where they can consult journals and reference books and draw exhibits? Will the curator allow responsible young people to handle material? These are just a few of the questions that pass through my mind. For most children a visit to a gallery means an hour with a worksheet finding the answers to a variety of questions. This is quite laudable if the teacher has geared the questions to the ability of the children, and there should be no problems, but there is always the difficulty of the lazy teacher who has not checked the displays and does not know that the Sutton Hoo treasure is on loan to Stockholm Museum or is using the worksheet with slow twelve-year-olds that was prepared for high-flying fifteen-year-olds. Such laziness can cause chaos on a visit and disturb other schools and visitors who are using the same area.

It is always a courtesy to inform a museum if you propose to take a large group of children, even if you do not want them to provide any special service. They may save you time by telling you that it will be closed on that day, or advising that the afternoon will be easier than the morning. It is always best to avoid the summer term when museums are heavily visited; October to March is much better, and you stand the chance of having the place to yourself. In June the Verulamium Museum gets as many as two thousand visiting children a week during school hours.

Publications stalls in museums can be most helpful to archaeology teachers, and stocks of relevant catalogues and offprints should be acquired to supplement the school's archaeological library. Colour slides and postcards can be purchased for follow-up or introductory work, and most museums will allow you to take your own photographs.

If a child becomes familiar with a museum at ten or eleven, by the time he reaches examination level he will have a good idea of its content and be able to choose clearly subjects for individual projects. Some parts of Britain have better local museum facilities than others. Some areas are museum blanks, whilst Wiltshire has at least four excellent archaeological collections. Details of the majority of museums can be found in the book *Museums and Galleries in Great Britain and Ireland* published annually by ABC Historic Publications. Telephone numbers are given and an enquiry will soon reveal whether there is an education officer who can help you with your visit.

What is the aim of the museum visit? It must be familiarisation with objects and materials of the past. For the archaeology student it is important to be able to recognise a beaker or a spindle whorl and that is what the visit will encourage; but is it enough? The answer must be 'No'. The student studying archaeology must be able to move beyond the recognition stage. He must be able to appreciate the way the object was made and used. This cannot be achieved simply by staring into a glass case. It is important to reconstruct the past technology associated with the object, and this leads us to one of the most useful aspects of teaching archaeology – imitative experiments.

10
Experimental archaeology

We cannot expect museums to lend us their best objects so that we can try to work out how they were used. But there is nothing to stop us making replicas of the objects and experimenting with those. There are a vast number of experiments that can be tried out.

A flint handaxe in a museum case tells us very little about the life of its maker and the way it was used. Yet flint is easy to come by, so why not attempt to copy it? This is not easy, and with inexperienced children it is dangerous, but using protective clothing, including leather gloves and goggles, students can make their first faltering attempts at flint knapping. First experiments will be concerned with finding the right stone or bone for a hammer, deciding on the right angle of blow, and detaching flakes in the desired direction. Replicating a particular handaxe takes tremendous skill and only a few specialists seem able to achieve it, but there is no problem in producing sharp flakes that can be used in a variety of cutting processes. At the same time children will learn something about the nature of flint and soon discover that surface material is inferior to that dug out of the chalk. They can also experiment with other varieties of stone to see which are suitable for cutting. Care should be taken to write up the experiment afterwards as a scientific record. The flint knapping exercise will produce sparks and ultimately fire. The children should find out how easy it is to light a fire without the use of matches.

Ask any student what would be his priorities if he found himself alone on a desert island. His answers would probably include finding food and water, building a hut and trying to make a boat. All these are good exercises in imitative archaeology. All would have presented any man with a challenge and we can only understand the difficulties if we are presented with them ourselves. A child's estimate of how long it would take to build a hut varies from an afternoon to a week. Admittedly it will depend on the sophistication of the structure. But here is an exercise well worth undertaking if the facilities are available, namely a building site, plenty of timber and roofing material. This suggests itself as a project for a rural school. Preferably the children will commence with the plan of an excavated hut and consider how best to reconstruct it. Peter Reynolds's books on iron age farms give all the necessary information. My own experiments with twenty

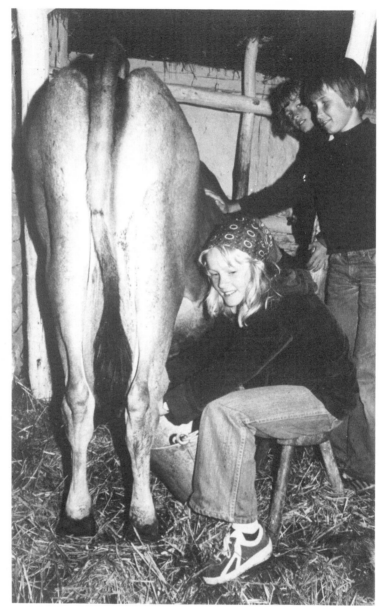

Plate 20. Is this archaeology? Milking a cow is as archaeological an activity as making a pot, and just as legitimate.

eleven-year-olds, using precut logs and modern digging equipment, took three days to build the framework and failed to complete either the walls or thatch. The general observation amongst the children was: 'Gosh, it takes much longer than you would think!'

Before pottery was invented it was difficult to boil food, but girls in particular may like to try a baking pit. A hole is dug into the ground about 10 inches (250 mm) deep and a yard (900 mm) in diameter. About fifty stones the size of medium apples are placed close at hand, and a fierce wood fire is started in the pit. This is kept going for about half an hour, after which it is stoked up and the stones are placed over the top. They are left for another half an hour until they are red-hot and then they are removed using wooden 'tongs', leaving only a layer of red-hot stones in the bottom of the pit. The material to be cooked, a piece of meat perhaps, wrapped in leaves (metal foil will substitute), is placed on the stones and the others are piled back over the top and covered with soil to retain the heat. The meat is left for as long as

Plate 21. A child practises weaving on a vertical loom.

Plate 22. Cooking by heating stones. The boy on the right is preparing a chicken for lunch.
Plate 23. Attempting to make bread using flour that they have ground themselves.

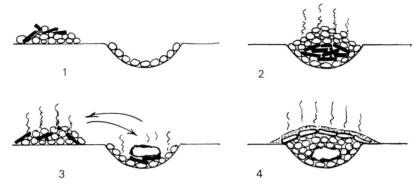

Fig. 1. Four stages in the development of a baking pit.

would be required to cook it in a normal oven. The baking pit can then be opened and the cooked meat removed. Care should be taken as very hot stones look quite cool in strong sunlight (fig. 1).

A most satisfying activity is the manufacture and firing of pottery. Pots of a coiled variety are easily made, and older children will adapt these to copy prehistoric examples. In most cases the vessels can be made from clay provided by the school's art department, but in geologically suitable areas it is worth digging for local clay, provided it does not contain too many stones. Comparison between vessels fired from local clay and pots in the local museum may show similar sources of material. Numerous books describe the making of simple pots. Firing can provide much interest and methods can be considered. The simplest method employs the open fire kiln (fig. 2). A shallow pit is dug and lined with many twigs placed radially. The dried pots are then laid on top of this, as close together as possible. A few wood shavings are placed amongst the pots for kindling. A cone of twigs is then built over the pots, and this is covered with a cone of

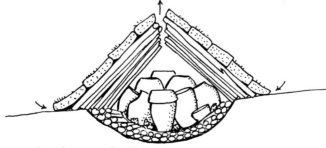

Fig. 2. Cross-section of an open fire kiln.

Plate 24. *(Above).* Experiments in making soup. The pots are replicas of iron age specimens.
Plate 25. *(Right)* Life in an iron age house. Children work around the central hearth in the experimental iron age village at Lejre in Denmark.

thicker wood. The fire can then be ignited and once the wood is burning turves are placed over the whole thing, leaving only a small hole for a draught at the top. Although the fire will burn out quite quickly, probably in less than an hour, it is best to leave it for half a day before carefully opening it, as the interior remains very hot, having reached a temperature of about 400 C (750 F). If plenty of air has found its way into the kiln the pots will come out with a reddish colour: black pots indicate that little oxygen was present.

The logical step from a simple kiln of this type is to try to reproduce an archaeologically excavated kiln. A number of schools have tried this experiment, and one of the most successful has been Hayfield Comprehensive School at Doncaster, where C. R. Fanthorpe, with assistance from G. F. Bryant, helped his CSE pupils to reconstruct a Romano-British above-ground turf-built pottery kiln with highly encouraging results, which they have published in a small booklet. Since then Hayfield has built a Roman-type single-flue kiln alongside a medieval-type three-flue for comparative purposes, keeping detailed records of every stage of their work.

During the pottery work, small shallow bowls can be made to be used as lamps, or alternatively blocks of chalk can be hollowed out to

produce a scoop the size of a small coffee cup. This is filled with pork dripping, into which a wick of dried grass or moss is placed. Lighting this with a spark from a flint is very difficult and the children may be permitted to cheat with matches! Lamps made from chalk or limestone blocks were used by palaeolithic man in the painted caves of France and Spain. I have always found that children enjoy trying to reproduce the methods of the cave artists in making their own pictures. If a plastered wall is available for painting so much the better; alternatively some obscure area like the ceiling of the cycle shed will do just as well. Stout sugar paper is a perfectly good substitute. The paint is made by mixing powdered ochre or prepared school powder paint with liquid fat, and it is applied to the work surface with paint brushes made by twisting the end of a green twig to produce a frayed end. Finger painting can also be tried, stippling with pads of moss or wool, or if the paint is sufficiently liquid it can be blown through a straw. These methods can also be used to produce a stencilled impression of a hand. Since the paint has a fat base, the pictures will take some time to dry.

The most satisfying examples of experimental archaeology are those which have a useful end product. One such includes the collection of wool and spinning of yarn, the dyeing of the skeins and the weaving of fabric. If possible children should be taken out into the fields during the spring to collect wool from hedges and barbed wire fences. A friendly sheep farmer may be persuaded to provide a little extra. It is then necessary to construct a simple hand-spindle and experiment with spinning. The spindle can be made by fixing a wooden disc on the end of a piece of dowel rod (fig. 3). The fleece is teased out into a soft mass like cotton wool. It is then rolled into a length of yarn and attached to the spindle. The fleece is held in the left hand whilst the spindle revolves in a clockwise direction between the right thumb and finger. As the spindle revolves, the hands close together and tease out the wool, which twists into yarn. As this increases in length it can be wound around the spindle. Once sufficient yarn has been produced it is normal to wash and dye it. Colouring can be achieved by experimenting with dyes made from berries and plant roots. There is not room in this book to describe the processes.

Construction of a full-size vertical loom is a fascinating project, although smaller scale replicas can also be made. My example is based on a Danish original reconstructed at Lejre and the working loom that can be seen in Taunton Museum. The diagram (fig. 4) shows all the component parts and suggests the approximate size of the timbers required. It will be noticed that the loom leans backwards in order to create a shed (or gap) between the alternate vertical warp

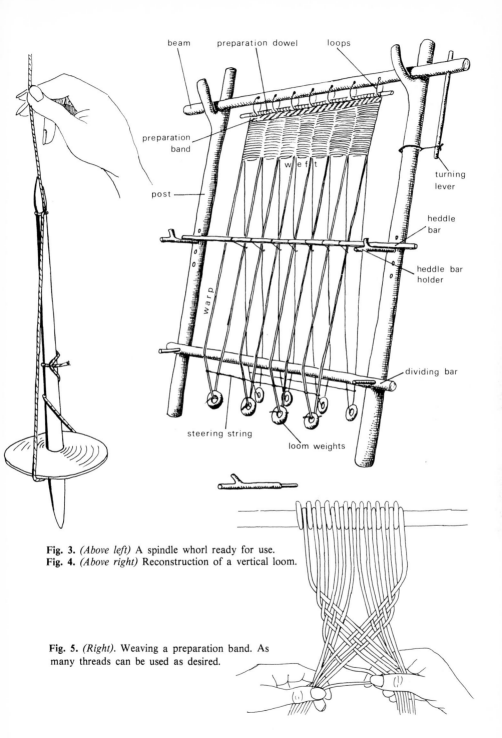

beam   preparation dowel   loops

preparation
band

post

w|e f|t

warp

turning
lever

heddle
bar

heddle bar
holder

dividing bar

steering string

loom weights

Fig. 3. *(Above left)* A spindle whorl ready for use.
Fig. 4. *(Above right)* Reconstruction of a vertical loom.

Fig. 5. *(Right).* Weaving a preparation band. As
many threads can be used as desired.

threads. By pulling the heddle bar backwards and forwards the shed can be reversed, making it possible to pass a shuttle carrying the horizontal weft threads from side to side. In starting the weaving it is necessary to weave a preparation band. This is a form of diagonal plaiting that has been known since the bronze age and is explained in fig. 5. The band can be made as broad as you wish and should be as long as the width of the fabric you want to weave. It is sewn to a row of small holes in the preparation dowel, and the warp threads hang down from it. These threads are weighted at the bottom by clay loom weights.

From the neolithic period onward man's life was dominated by farming. Consequently it is not surprising that we should concern ourselves with agricultural experiments, which may be tried by even the youngest children. A piece of rough ground can be cleared by the slash and burn technique. Digging sticks, with clay or stone weights, can be used with varying success, and examples of hoes can be made by attaching roughly rectangular flints or other stones to the split ends of sticks. Binding with leather thongs will keep them in place. Sowing seed corn by scattering from a basket and raking with leafy branches are exercises that can be tried even in urban gardens. But perhaps most fun can be obtained by producing food which the children can actually consume. Whilst it is possible to eat a wide variety of wild plants, and prehistoric man certainly used them for food and medicine, it is best to stick to those foods whose safety is known.

Milking animals may not seem like experimental archaeology, but cattle, goats and sheep provided milk as a staple drink and food for early man, and man had to learn to handle the beasts. Milk-based foods are an obvious choice for experiment. Butter can be made by skimming the cream off a large dish of milk which has stood overnight in a cool room. The cream should then be whipped in a dish for about an hour, using a whisk made of twigs. The butter will need to be salted and the buttermilk removed. About 9 pints (5 litres) of fresh milk are required to produce half a pound (225 grams) of butter.

Cottage cheese is prepared by placing milk in a large bowl at room temperature and adding a little sour milk. After two days the milk separates into thick curds and liquid whey. Pour off the whey and then add salt to the curds and sieve it through muslin. Press the curd to remove as much of the remaining whey as possible. The cheese should then be placed in a cool place for some weeks to mature, preferably with a weight on it, and it will be ready for eating when it meets the taste of the maker.

Grain was grown in some quantity, though often mixed with the seeds of weeds which got combined into the food. Children can attempt to grind corn by adapting the saddle quern method of rubbing a small stone on to a flat, larger one. A co-operative museum may even loan a real quern or Roman mortarium for the purpose. Small bread rolls can be made by mixing ground flour with a little sour milk or buttermilk and a pinch of salt. Shaped into rolls, they can be baked in a hot oven for half an hour, or more realistically in the hot cinders of a fire (wrapped in foil).

Oat cakes are made by mixing crushed oats and milk or water with a pinch of salt. This is kneaded and rolled into little balls which are flattened out and baked on hot flat stones beside a fire. Honey and nuts can be added for variety.

Porridge is made by boiling coarsely ground barley with milk or water and salt, until it is tender. It can be sweetened with honey and made more interesting by adding pieces of apple or other fruit.

Although early man grew many of his own crops, he must often have relied on natural varieties. A number of these can safely be used for cooking and often have places in traditional remedy books. Nettles, yarrow, wild carrot, horsetail, wood sorrel, dock, mugwort, angelica and thyme can all be used in a variety of ways. Boiled water poured on to the dried leaves of mugwort, for example, produces a tea-like infusion. The wide variety of fungi should also be remembered and respected, since many are very poisonous.

Prehistoric man was also a hunter and would have killed many of the wild animals, birds and fish that were found near his home. He also killed surplus farm animals and all these provided a plentiful food supply. Children can experiment with the cooking of meat, starting simply by barbecuing sausages or chickens. Such cooking involves working with fire and will need careful supervision. Try to keep the flames under a foot high, and never use flammable liquids or paper to light the fire. The sticks should be about $1\frac{1}{2}$ inches (40 mm) in diameter, arranged in a cone, with larger dried logs outside providing the flames. To cook meat it should first be salted and spiced with mint or wormwood and then wrapped in plenty of large leaves (metal foil could substitute). Then it should be placed in a glowing fire, covered with hot charcoal and left for about an hour for every 2 pounds (900 grams) weight of meat. Thin cuts of meat and fish can also be grilled on hot slabs of stone placed close to the fire.

A number of experiments of the kind described in this section can be seen at the Butser Ancient Farm Project in Hampshire, and any school within easy reach of the centre is strongly recommended to make a visit (see page 61).

11
Excavation and extra-mural activities

For most people archaeology means excavation. To young children archaeology is about digging up the past, and archaeologists are old men with thin grey hair called professors. At the time of writing it is remarkable how many professors of archaeology are young men with vigorous hair growth who do very little excavating. Certainly excavation is the traditional method of obtaining our basic information in archaeology, but, rather like surgery, it tends to be used as a last resort. All excavation is destructive. It has taken more than a hundred years for us to appreciate this, and now excavation is normally only undertaken when a site would otherwise be destroyed, or when some vital piece of information can only be obtained by digging. As a result we have today rescue and research excavations, of which the former are by far the most common. As their name implies rescue excavations are carried out when a site is likely to be destroyed by a motorway, factory or some other major earthmoving activity. Usually such excavations are financed by the government through the Department of the Environment, or a local archaeological unit often attached to the county planning office or some other responsible body. Some of the larger county archaeological societies, museums and universities may also sponsor rescue excavations. Whoever is responsible must recognise that excavation is a highly skilled operation and it can only be undertaken by a carefully trained staff. However, it is not yet a closed shop and anyone with a genuine interest will usually find a welcome on a site and can join in the work under supervision.

Your local museum will tell you if there are any excavations close at hand. If not the CBA *Calendar of Excavations* is published six times a year from April to September with details of digs where volunteers are welcome. Normally children are expected to be sixteen before they can join an excavation, but if a teacher is with them, or a letter of recommendation is sent to the director, slightly younger children will often be accepted. From the start it must be made clear to anyone joining a dig for the first time that they should not expect to begin with a top job. Turfing or moving topsoil for three days may well be the prelude to less exhausting work and will kill the ardour of many budding enthusiasts in the process.

The teacher planning to take children on an excavation will have to consider all the implications. There is an element of danger and the children will need to be insured. Whilst some excavators offer all meals and accommodation others only offer a camping site. This latter poses the responsibility of seeing that the children are properly fed, clean and in good health. Leaking tents and food poisoning are common disasters that may have to be met. A mixed party of boys and girls will need male and female staff for supervision; indeed few excavation directors would accept children without. On the site the teachers would be expected to observe reasonably strict discipline. The archaeologists have a job to do in limited time, and they do not want their plans disorganised by a rabble of indisciplined children. Such badly behaved children would inevitably prejudice the chances of others being taken on future digs.

When the teacher cannot accompany children, he should be satisfied in his own mind that youngsters he is sending to a dig are responsible, sensible people who will respect what they are doing. A teacher should never recommend someone to dig if he is not as certain as possible of the child's integrity. Even so, someone will often let him down. I would be unhappy to recommend all but a few children under fifteen unless the director is experienced in handling young children.

Does this mean that children under fifteen cannot excavate? Not necessarily, but it should be stressed time and again that no one, child or adult, should excavate on his own, especially if he has not been properly trained. And training does not mean taking part in one dig; it means at least a fortnight on each of a dozen, before one can think of working on one's own.

There are two things a teacher can do to simulate an excavation. One suitable for the youngest children is to bury objects in a deep sand tray and to proceed to excavate these following the basic excavation techniques, and recording exactly what is found. On a larger scale the same exercise can be tried in the school jumping pit, provided the PE teacher has agreed and no dangerous objects are buried in the sand (e.g. glass bottles). Perhaps the best answer was found by a school that had been built on a filled-in rubbish dump. They dug into the corner of the school playing field and produced a trench with a superb section of stratified rubbish twenty years old. There is nothing to stop other teachers seeking out old rubbish tips and obtaining permission to dig, but care should be taken if the material is loosely packed that it will not collapse. A Victorian rubbish tip is best if one can be located. A class of junior school children excavated the site of a Second World War air-raid shelter that was going to be destroyed in their teacher's back garden. He knew it was there, they did not, and they had not only to uncover it, but to try to interpret what they had found. With a little help from parents they reached a satisfactory conclusion, producing a report and display of their finds. Something of a similar nature might be tried on the site of a demolished house or barn.

This chapter may prove frustrating to the teacher with young children and no rubbish dump or collapsed air-raid shelter near their school. I would remind them of what I have said about field walking as an alternative and satisfying activity in a rural area.

There can be few schools where there is not an archaeological monument of some kind within reasonable distance. This may be a site of national importance in the care of the Department of the Environment, or it may be a simple moated homestead or plough-torn burial mound. With a little knowledge the teacher should be able to devise some exercise suitable for the ability of his class.

Almost all sites offer opportunities for elementary survey work. Good plans may exist of the earthwork, but it is surprising how often they do not. Exercises in triangulation using simple paced measurements or accurate measuring tapes are all very worthwhile. The teacher will need to know something about the techniques, and good background information is available in *Survey by Prismatic Compass* by R. A. H. Farrar (CBA) and the more detailed *Surveying for Archaeologists and other Fieldworkers* by A. H. A. Hogg (Croom Helm). If good ground plans are produced they should be supplemented by written notes and photographs of any features not otherwise recorded, like exposures of drystone walling or signs of burning. Sections of earthworks should be included where possible and this will involve the student in learning to level. On completion a copy of the work should be deposited with the local Sites and Monuments Record. After the careful survey of a hillfort an attempt can be made to calculate the amount of work involved in its construction and the approximate time taken. The author has produced such calculations in his book *Hillforts of England and Wales,* published in this series. I have already mentioned children storming the ramparts of a hillfort. They might also experiment with firing sling stones and calculating their range. The next logical step is to attempt to build a contour model of the site, perhaps out of polystyrene or plaster, and this will lead to reconstruction drawings and models. In a suitably equipped school, children might try to reconstruct part of the bank and ditch of a hillfort full size. Long barrows like Belas Knap and Nympsfield are ideal subjects for modelmaking, which again begins with survey work in the field. The orthostats can be made from actual stones or modelled in clay or plasticine. If covered with sand or fine earth the site can be actually 'excavated'. I recall one crazy winter in which children built a model of Stonehenge out of snow, which was easier to explain as educational than building a snowman!

Stone circles offer opportunities for considering the astronomical alignments of such sites. To do this properly the teacher needs some astronomical knowledge, otherwise his results are likely to be as inconclusive as those of the writer and a group of children who spent a futile hour in the moonlight at Rollright trying to align the stones with various stars. The only positive result was some blunt and imaginative writing from the children next day.

In recent years the so-called industrial archaeology has become tagged on to legitimate archaeology. Whilst it purports to be the study of buildings and objects connected with industry both in the past and present, it is really much wider and would be better called historical archaeology. It deals with historical problems from an archaeological viewpoint and can be used to sort out the history of a church, a row of houses or a churchyard. All these latter ideas are readily adapted to an urban area where children can either begin with the oldest building in their locality, usually the church, and with the aid of a knowledgeable teacher and a copy of Pevsner attempt to unravel the periods of construction. Using early maps, directories and architectural guides they can discover the former function of terraces of houses and factories, used perhaps for hat manufacture or lacemaking. Best of all a graveyard survey will provide the names and history of a parish often for the past two hundred years, especially if Jeremy Jones's excellent booklet *How to Record Graveyards* (CBA) is consulted for ideas. Churchyard surveys can either be carried out by a group of children or by individuals. Care must first be taken to obtain permission, and then simple sketch plans can be prepared for general identification purposes. A detailed survey can be carried out later. The basic idea is to make an accurate record of each inscription where it is still legible. This can be made easier by using the record cards prepared by the CBA. Each tombstone is numbered, photographed and the inscriptions copied. In a survey at Stondon in Bedfordshire photographs were taken with flash bulbs at an oblique angle to the stone, providing excellent results. The purpose of the survey is not only to make a record of something which is being destroyed by time and weathering, but also to add to the history of the parish. Family trees can be compiled, average age at death worked out, infant mortality figures collated, and so on. By comparing the names found with the records of burials in the parish register, it will be seen that only a tiny fraction of the deceased actually had

Plate 26. Recording the details of a tombstone for a graveyard survey.

gravestones. Most went uncommemorated. Perhaps there is a lesson to be learnt here for students of prehistoric burial methods.

When the writer was fifteen he started a school archaeological society. A friendly history teacher gave his support but could offer no archaeology. The local museum curator started us off with a lecture on the locality, but after that the writer was on his own, and many evenings that should have been allotted to homework were devoted to preparing next week's lecture and visual aids. Today's children will probably have a society or club formed for them by a sympathetic teacher. Whilst some of its activities may consist of illustrated talks, it is probable that visits and experimental work will be carried out. The advantage of an archaeological society is that it will attract the pupils with genuine interest and enthusiasm for carrying through projects to a logical conclusion. Societies or clubs can be run on different levels catering for all the age groups. At Duxford Church of England Primary School Miss Frances Dale has run a successful club since 1975 with thirty children of mixed ability meeting fortnightly in school time for an hour and a quarter. With help from parents, children have experienced field walking, simple surveying, graveyard recording and architectural recognition. Indoors they have produced projects and models and familiarised themselves with a wealth of objects loaned by museums, as well as experimenting with dyeing and weaving. Older children in other schools have also followed similar themes at a deeper level, practising land clearance and experiments in early agriculture, building kilns and smelting furnaces, or writing parish archaeologies by studying museum records and collections. The school archaeological society is ideal for the teacher with an archaeological interest, especially if he is not permitted to teach the subject on the timetable but has sufficient enthusiasm to want to share it with the children. After-school activities, weekend visits, cycle tours using youth hostels and holiday excavations all become possible under the guidance of this valuable member of staff.

Some of the older public schools have had archaeological societies for years, and a number have their own museums. Very often the classics teacher finds himself in charge of the museum and the success of the venture will depend on his interest. School museums have a habit of attracting a wide range of exhibits extending from local Roman pottery to a mummified crocodile presented by an old boy. At worst the museum is a jackdaw collection of bric-a-brac: at best, a valuable teaching aid, well housed and scrupulously labelled and cared for. The sad thing about school museums is that they often attract valuable local material which is safe whilst looked after by a good curator, but as soon as that teacher leaves, or there is a change in the use of the school, the whole collection can get neglected and disseminated. A valuable collection of Saxon jewellery in a Bedfordshire school museum vanished without trace over a period of ten years. For this reason the author would advocate a series of temporary exhibitions on specific themes, with material borrowed for a short period from pupils and friends, rather than a fully operational museum, unless curatorial duties are written in to a teacher's contract and proper access is available not only to pupils, but to all genuinely interested scholars at reasonable times from all walks of life. The collection will need to be securely locked and guarded and properly insured. Few schools can satisfy these requirements and in most cases school museums should be actively discouraged.

12
Further information

Anyone interested in British archaeology will soon discover that the most important address is that of the Council for British Archaeology, 112 Kennington Road, London SE11 6RE (telephone 01-582 0494). Most information is centralised at that address, and the CBA is responsible for many useful publications including the *Calendar of Excavations, Archaeological Abstracts* and the *Archaeological Resources Handbook for Teachers*. This latter publication, produced by the Schools Committee of the CBA, is invaluable for anyone teaching archaeology. The Schools Committee also produces a series of *Bulletins of Archaeology for Schools* and other helpful literature, details of which can be obtained on application to the Education Officer. A number of articles from these *Bulletins* have been recently reprinted in a set of booklets called *Archaeology for Schools*.

Government controlled archaeology in Britain is administered by the Department of the Environment, which also has an educational service. Enquiries should be made to the Education Officer, Directorate of Ancient Monuments and Historic Buildings, Department of the Environment, Room 105, 25 Savile Row, London W1X 2BT (01-734 6010).

The Young Archaeologists Club is run for children by Dr Kate Pretty, New Hall, Cambridge. For a small annual subscription children receive a magazine and information about new discoveries, competitions and sites that they can visit.

Teachers wanting up-to-date information are advised to contact *Archeology in Education*, Department of Prehistory and Archaeology, the University of Sheffield. They should also join one of the learned archaeological societies, such as the following:

Royal Archaeological Institute, 304 Addison House, Grove End Road, London NW8 9EL. Annual subscription allows access to the Society of Antiquaries Library at Burlington House, London.

The Prehistoric Society, Harvest House, 62 London Road, Reading, RG1 5AS.

Society for the Promotion of Roman Studies, 31-4 Gordon Square, London WC1H 0PP. Annual subscription includes one of two journals: *Journal of Roman Studies* and *Britannia*.

Society for Medieval Archaeology, Harvest House, 62 London Road, Reading, RG1 5AS.

Three periodicals of a generalised nature will keep teachers up to date with happenings in the archaeological world:
Antiquity, c/o Heffers Printers Ltd, King's Hedges Road, Cambridge, CB4 2PQ. Three issues per year.
Current Archaeology, 9 Nassington Road, London NW3 2TX. Six issues a year.
Popular Archaeology, 24 Barton Street, Bath. Twelve issues a year.
   Details of examinations in archaeology can be obtained from the relevant examination boards:
CSE. Only Mode 3 examinations are available. A specimen syllabus is available from the CBA.
A/O Level: University of London, University Entrance and School Examinations Council, 66-72 Gower Street, London WC1E 6EE, or Joint Matriculation Board, Manchester, M15 6EU.
A Level. Cambridge University Local Examinations Syndicate, Syndicate Buildings, 17 Harvey Road, Cambridge, CB1 2EU.
   Teachers wishing to purchase aerial photographs are advised first to contact their local museum or archaeological unit to see what material is available. The most important educational source of aerial photographs is the Committee for Aerial Photography, Mond Building, Free School Lane, Cambridge, CB2 3RF. The major commercial source is Aerofilms Ltd, Gate Studios, Station Road, Boreham Wood, Hertfordshire, WD6 1EJ. In all cases when ordering aerial photographs, as much detail should be given as possible to locate the site, including local names and national grid references.
   Slides of archaeological sites are available from the Department of the Environment. A number of commercial companies produce filmstrips, many of which can be cut up and mounted as 35 mm slides. The leading filmstrip manufacturer is Visual Publications, 197 Kensington High Street, London W8 6BB, who will supply catalogues and preview material upon request. Many local museums also produce visual material, which the teacher will discover by patient search.
   Teachers in the south of England may like to visit the Butser Ancient Farm Project in Hampshire. Enquiries should be addressed to the project at Rookham Lodge, East Meon, Hampshire: telephone, during office hours, Hambledon (070 132) 386.
   Teachers needing local help should contact their nearest museum or archaeological unit. The latter is often situated in the County Planning Department or museum.

13
A basic library
for teachers

Barker, P. *Techniques of Archaeological Excavation.* Batsford, 1977.
Beresford, M. W. and Hurst, J. G. *Deserted Medieval Villages.* Lutterworth, 1971.
Brown, D. *Anglo-Saxon England.* Bodley Head, 1978.
Burgess, C. *The Age of Stonehenge.* Dent, 1980.
Burl, A. *Prehistoric Avebury.* Yale University Press, 1979.
Campbell, J. (editor). *The Anglo-Saxons.* Phaidon, 1982.
Coles, J. *Field Archaeology in Britain.* Methuen, 1972.
Coles, J. *Experimental Archaeology.* Academic Press, 1979.
Cossons, N. *The BP Book of Industrial Archaeology.* David and Charles, 1975.
Cunliffe, B. *Iron Age Communities in Britain.* Routledge and Kegan Paul, 1978.
Dyer, J. *Discovering Archaeology in England and Wales.* Shire, 1980.
Dyer, J. *Penguin Guide to Prehistoric England and Wales.* Penguin, 1982.
Fasham, P. J. *et al. Fieldwalking for Archaeologists.* Hampshire Field Club, 1980.
Foote, P. and Wilson, D. M. *The Viking Achievement.* Sidgwick and Jackson, 1980.
Frere, S. *Britannia.* Routledge and Kegan Paul, 1978.
Jones, G. *A History of the Vikings.* Oxford, 1968.
Major, J. K. *Fieldwork in Industrial Archaeology.* Batsford, 1975.
Megaw, V. and Simpson, D. *Introduction to British Prehistory.* Leicester University Press, 1979.
Muir, R. *Shell Guide to Reading the Landscape.* Michael Joseph, 1981.
Platt, C. *Medieval England.* Routledge and Kegan Paul, 1978.
Renfrew, C. *British Prehistory.* Duckworth, 1974.
Renn, D. *Norman Castles in Britain.* John Baker, 1968.
Reynolds, P. *Iron Age Farm.* Colonnade, 1979.
Taylor, C. *Fieldwork in Medieval Archaeology.* Batsford, 1974.
Wacher, J. *Roman Britain.* Batsford, 1980.
Wilson, D. M. (editor). *The Archaeology of Anglo-Saxon England.* Methuen, 1976.

Wood, E. S. *Collins Field Guide to Archaeology.* Collins, 1979.
Wymer, J. *The Palaeolithic Age.* Croom Helm, 1982.

The inexpensive *Shire Archaeology* series is produced with teachers and students very much in mind. A wide selection of titles is available, listed on the back cover, and the series is being constantly enlarged and revised. Shire also publish an extensive list of industrial archaeology titles. Catalogues are available upon request.

Plate 27. Even three-year-old children can perform a valuable task given the opportunity.

Index